HEART AND SOUL

The Story of America and African Americans

HEART AND SOUL

The Story of America and African Americans

Words and paintings by

KADIR NELSON

Balzer + Bray | An Imprint of HarperCollinsPublishers

I would like to thank all of those who helped with the creation of Heart and Soul: *my grandmother, Verlee Gunter-Moore; my mother, Emily Gunter; Shermaine Gary; Olivia Morris; Barbara Brown; William Ricks; Walter McCoy; Debra and Darrell Gunter; Faye Robinson; Cynthia Robinson-Gordon; Gaynell Taylor; James Taylor; Dr. DeAnna Burt; and Cinque Henderson. A huge thank-you to my right hand and superstar editor, Donna Bray; my brilliant designer, Martha Rago; copyeditor Maggie Herold; Professor Jill Watts; my super agent, Steven Malk, and Writers House; Ruta Rimas; and my wife, Keara, and children, Amel, Aya, and Ali. A very special thank-you to all of those at HarperCollins who believed in this book and to the authors and filmmakers whose work has inspired my love of history, namely Dr. Henry Louis Gates Jr., Dr. John Hope Franklin, Howard Zinn, and Ken Burns.*

Balzer + Bray is an imprint of HarperCollins Publishers.

Heart and Soul: The Story of America and African Americans
Copyright © 2011 by Kadir Nelson
Excerpt, pp. 15 and 18, from *The Interesting Narrative and Other Writings* by Olaudah Equiano, pp. 47–59.
Story about boy on bus, p. 83, adapted from *The History Channel Presents: Voices of the Civil Rights Movement* DVD.

Library of Congress Cataloging-in-Publication Data

Nelson, Kadir.
 Heart and soul : the story of America and African Americans / by Kadir Nelson. — 1st ed.
  p. cm.
 ISBN 978-0-06-173079-5 (pbk.)
 1. African Americans—History—Juvenile literature. 2. United States—Civilization—African American influences—Juvenile literature. I. Title.

E185.N427 2011   2010046236
973'.0496073—dc22   CIP
                                                                          AC

Typography by Martha Rago
20 21 LSCW 14
❖
First paperback edition, 2014

For my family:
the Reaveses, the Pittmans, the Nelsons, the Hardys, the Wrights, and the Gunters;
and for every American family whose invaluable contributions and stories have
helped stitch the grand quilt of these United States.

PROLOGUE

*M*ost folks my age and complexion don't speak much about the past. Sometimes it's just too hard to talk about—nothing we like to share with you young folk. No parent wants to tell a child that he was once a slave and made to do another man's bidding. Or that she had to swallow her pride and take what she was given, even though she knew it wasn't fair. Our story is chock-full of things like this. Things that might make you cringe, or feel angry. But there are also parts that will make you proud, or even laugh a little. You gotta take the good with the bad, I guess. You have to know where you come from so you can move forward.

Many of us are getting up in age and feel it's time to make some things known before they are gone for good. So it's important that you pay attention, honey, because I'm only going to tell you this story but once.

1

DECLARATIONS OF INDEPENDENCE

"Liberty, when it begins to take root, is a plant of rapid growth." —George Washington

Ever visit the Capitol in Washington, DC? It's a beautiful white building made of sandstone, and it has a *big* iron dome that rises over the city like a full moon. It was built by slaves and freemen to be a symbol of the liberty Americans had won from England in the American Revolution. Inside the rotunda there are large paintings and sculptures of famous Americans. Big ol' statues of Abraham Lincoln and George Washington. The paintings tell the story of how America came to be. Strange though . . . nary a black face in all of those pretty pictures. There's plenty of white folks and a few Indians here and there, but none of us. It's as if we never existed—stricken from the record, like Moses from the walls of Egypt. Of course, those fancy paintings ain't telling the whole truth. Black folks have been here at least as long as Europeans. By the early 1600s, English, Spanish, Portuguese, Dutch, and French settlers had made their way to America and established colonies all along the East Coast. The colonies were a means for European countries to expand their empires and were also a new source of wealth. Each colony produced crops and mined for riches that were sent back to Europe. Africans had come to America as laborers with the Spanish

The Baptism of Pocahontas *by John Gadsby Chapman, Capitol rotunda, Washington, DC* in Florida in 1565, and about sixty years later with the English in Virginia, to do the work of building the colonies and producing what was sent back to Europe. The labor of these Africans helped to create the foundation of America in its early days. So you see, we deserved to be in those pictures just as much as the Europeans and Indians. And if you really want to know the truth, honey, *we* are much of the reason they would later have a chance to fight for their "liberty" in the first place.

By the mid 1700s, the English colonists had been in America for a few generations. They had gained control of most of the settled land along the eastern seaboard, set up local governments, and made the colonies quite profitable by way of slave-produced crops. Having been in America for so long, many of the colonists had come to think of themselves as American rather than British and had grown good and tired of living under the thumb of a faraway king. The colonists felt it was time they had a say about how they ran their local governments. They began to talk on the streets, over dinner tables, and in taverns about the king's unfair taxes, about his nosy soldiers everywhere, and about splitting from England. They talked about not wanting to be *slaves* to the king. Slaves? Chile, what in the world could they *ever* know about that?

The king had taxed the colonists for everything from paint to glass and paper. He even taxed their tea. People in the colonies had finally had enough. To show the king what they thought of his taxes, they snuck out to his boats and dumped all of his tea into the harbor. It wasn't long before the king sent more troops over here to try to put the folks in the colonies back in their place. But it only made relations worse, and the colonists more determined than ever to split with England. In two years, there was blood on the streets of Boston. And in one more, Thomas Jefferson wrote the Declaration of Independence to cut ties with England. The American Revolution had begun.

There were slaves who fought in that war, but unfortunately, many of them chose the wrong side. By the time of the Revolutionary War, there were more than 450,000 black folks, both slave and free, in the colonies. The British had promised freedom to any slave who fought for them—and, honey, that was a powerful thing to tell a slave—so thousands of them joined the British. General George Washington, who was in charge of the American troops, didn't allow black folks in his army. He and the Congress didn't think it was a good idea to put guns in the hands of folks who might well use them against their former masters or other white folks.

Revolutionary War soldier

But Washington changed his mind after he had lost so many of his soldiers to fighting and the pox. Only then were free black folks and some of the slaves allowed to join his army. General Washington was quickly rewarded by all the black men who signed up to help him gain the upper hand.

After eight years of war, America won its freedom from England and its citizens were able to manage their own affairs and control their property without having to pay the crown for the privilege. Oh, did I mention that their "property" included us? Both the slaves and free black folks who fought in this war for "freedom" hoped that the government might free *all* the slaves in the colonies if they fought for them, but the government only freed the people who fought in the army and slaves who lived in New England states like Massachusetts that chose to abolish slavery after the war. Just about everybody else was out of luck—especially many of the slaves who fought for the British. Some left with the British or fled to Canada, but most went right back into slavery.

A few years later, America wrote her founding papers, the Constitution; George Washington was made the very first president; and a new country was born. It should have been a proud moment for everybody, but, honey, we didn't have much reason to celebrate. Through the fruits of our labor and our volunteer soldiers, we had helped free America from England, and yet we were stuck in a country that kept most of us as slaves.

President George Washington and slave, Mount Vernon, Virginia

2

SLAVERY

"Dem days was hell." —Delia Garlic, former slave, Alabama

This may sound funny to you, but my grandfather, Joseph, didn't allow any of his kin to eat black-eyed peas on New Year's Day even though it's an old African American tradition—the beans bring good luck for the coming year, they say. But Pap, which is what we called him, wouldn't hear of it. When he was a young boy, each New Year's Day buckets of black-eyed peas were boiled and poured into a horse trough for all of the slaves on the plantation to eat like animals. Pap hated it and vowed that none of us in his family would ever allow people to treat us that way.

Pap was the only Africa-born slave in my family. Pap was captured in 1850 when he was only six years old, and brought to America. Even though it had been illegal to capture and import slaves to America since 1807, it still happened. And often. On New Year's Day of every year, Pap told us the story.

"When I was a child, I would play with all de other children in my village while de grown folk were working far away in de fields. They told us to look out for kidnappers 'cause dey were stories of people who went missing, mostly

Young Pap

children left at home during de day. One day when de grown folk were gone out to de field, several of dos people ran into de village carrying nets and clubs and grabbed me and several other children 'fore we could cry out. Dey covered our mouths, tied our hands, and ran off with us into de woods."

The children were marched for miles all the way to the coast, where a large ship sat out on the water. For days Pap and many other captured Africans were kept inside a large fort on the beach before they were brought outside and paddled in a small boat to the ship.

Below the deck, African men, women, and children were packed like fish, chained together, and crammed into spaces so tight that they could not stand up. It was dark, and the air was heavy with the smell of sickness and the cries of women and children. When the ship was full, it set off for America.

The trip lasted several weeks. Pap was sold to a planter in Maryland as a playmate for his son. When he reached the age of seven, Pap was sent out to work as a field hand.

I could tell you about the life of a slave all day long, but even then you couldn't guess the awfulness of it. Slaves are people who are property of *other* people and must do whatever they are told. They were bought and sold as one would buy and sell any animal or thing. Slaves had no right to property, to family, to come and go as they pleased, to read or write, or to speak their own language or have a last name; no right even to protect themselves—no more rights than that of a horse or a pig. The only right a slave had was to work for his master. And work he did.

Every morning the slave driver blew the work horn or rang the bell; and all the slaves woke up, grabbed a hoe, and headed out to the fields. In the summertime the sun was up early and down late; and the air was hot, heavy, and full of mosquitoes. With each strike of the hoe to the ground the slaves sang to keep time with each other and help ease the hard work. Spirituals were born right there in that field, you know. Singing was the only way to keep from dying inside. Pap said it was the saddest thing in the world to hear slaves sing those songs, but it sounded so beautiful. Made him want to cry. Some of those songs held secrets, too—codes to pass on messages to other slaves right under the nose of the overseer. Like when a slave started singing "Steal Away," folks knew it was time to run away. Or when they sang "Follow the Drinking Gourd," the slaves knew to escape in the direction of the North Star right at the foot of the Little Dipper.

Tobacco field

To ease the trouble of their hard lives, the slaves got together and danced on Saturday evenings. Most other evenings they slipped off into the woods for prayer meetings, praying for the day that freedom would come.

Since Pap didn't have any blood family on the plantation, older slaves took him in as their own. Before he went out to the fields, he lived in the big house with a woman he called Aunt Hattie, who worked all day under the watchful eye of the Missus, cooking, cleaning, sewing, even nursing the Missus's children when they needed milk. She raised all three of the Missus's children.

There were about a hundred or so slaves on the plantation, and they were always hungry and dressed in rags. Most of them went barefoot 'cause the master didn't give 'em but one pair of shoes a year, and the shoes weren't made to last. In the fields they were watched over by an overseer, who rode around on a horse making sure everybody was doing their work. And, honey, that fellow was mean. To keep the slaves in line, he lashed them with a curlin' bullwhip he kept on his shoulder. Tied 'em to a tree and whipped 'em right in front of all the other field hands. Folks a mile away could hear them awful whippings. It's no wonder so many of the slaves wanted to run away.

You might wonder, "Why didn't they fight back?" Chile, believe me when I tell you that they did, every step of the way; but unlike their fellow Africans who captured them, they didn't have any guns to fight back with, so they fought with their fists and died. They fought over the ocean on slave ships and were shot and drowned. They fought in the fields, in homes, and in factories where they worked and were whipped, beaten, and murdered. They fought and fought and lost almost every time. It would be a long while before we figured out that we could not win our freedom with our fists or guns. We would have to find another way.

Whipping tree

3

ABOLITION

"That which is not just is not law."
—William Lloyd Garrison, abolitionist

"I expose slavery in this country, because to expose it is to kill it." —Frederick Douglass, abolitionist

Even though it didn't specifically say so, slavery was written into the new Constitution right along with "We the People." The framers, who wrote the Constitution, could have ended slavery right then and there if they wanted to, and they even thought about it, but instead they chose to keep it. They thought they needed it. You see, America grew up on slavery. It was like mother's milk to the new country, and it made her grow big and strong. Southern planters had lined their pockets with profits from slave-grown crops, and northern industries depended on them too.

To justify slavery, southern white folks had convinced themselves that black people were fine with being slaves. We were convinced that they were all nuts or, as we would say, "touched in the head." Not a one of them would have traded places with us. And since those white gentlemen running the country wouldn't give us our freedom, we decided to take it ourselves.

Cleaned cotton

One of the slaves on Pap's plantation had taught himself to read, which was *very* dangerous, because if white folks had found out, he would have got a sound licking. White folks thought that if slaves learned to read or write, they could read the Bible for themselves or antislavery papers (if they got their hands on them) and begin to question their master's behavior. They might also be able to communicate with other slaves and antislavery folks outside of their plantations. Education is a powerful thing and often made slaves hard to control and likely to run away, so their masters took good care to make sure they remained illiterate. In fact, at the time it was illegal for slaves to read or write. A lot of them learned anyway. They'd trick their young masters into teaching them the alphabet or find a spelling book and sneak off to learn it and then teach the other slaves.

As it turns out, white folks were right about slaves who learned to read. That boy from Pap's plantation eventually ran away to Massachusetts, where he became a great speaker, talking to large crowds of white folks about how terrible it was to be a slave. He also wrote a narrative about his life that made him very famous. Many came to know him as "the Lion of Anacostia." Pap knew him as Frederick Douglass.

Up North, Douglass joined with other free black folks, former slaves, and good white folks who were trying to end slavery. They were called abolitionists because they wanted to *abolish* slavery. Abolitionists were everywhere, even in the South. They worked with folks like Harriet Tubman to help slaves escape to the North by way of the Underground Railroad—not a real railroad, but a loose network of safe houses and secret routes. Preaching about the awfulness of slavery was one of the best ways to fight it, and Douglass and Tubman did their best to spread the gospel. They lit a fire inside many a slave to take their freedom.

But it was a hard row to hoe. Even though slavery was dying out up North, it was getting stronger down South. Cotton was the most profitable crop in the country, and plenty of slaves were needed to grow it. To meet the demand for more cotton, tens of thousands of slaves in northern slave states were marched hundreds of miles on foot out west and down the Mississippi River into the Deep South. Pap remembered seeing a group of them tied together like horses to a wagon, marching down the road past his plantation.

New states were being added all the time as Americans started settling the West. Congress would determine whether or not each new state should allow slavery, and it was *always* a fight. As the country grew in

Frederick Douglass

size, so did the tension between North and South. Then in 1854, Congress passed the Kansas-Nebraska Act, which left it up to the settlers of the new territories to decide whether or not to allow slavery. The new law allowed slavery to exist *above* the Mason-Dixon Line, the symbolic dividing line between North and South at the border of Maryland and Pennsylvania, which was drawn thirty-four years prior during the Missouri Compromise. This scared the pants off of antislavery folks, because the compromise made it so that slavery would be limited to the South. But now slavery seemed to be on the move. It put a fire in the bellies of abolition folks all over the Union, including a country lawyer named Abraham Lincoln. Because of it, that fellow decided to run for president.

Southern white folks couldn't stand Lincoln. He had often spoken out against the spread of slavery; and southerners were convinced that if he were elected president, it would spell the end to their way of life. It's no wonder why slaves and free black folks took an instant liking to the country lawyer. In him, they saw a chance to put an end to slavery for good. The truth, though, was that Lincoln didn't have any intentions of abolishing slavery and very publicly said as much. But southerners didn't believe him.

Slaves on Pap's plantation were following the election closely, eavesdropping on white folks in the streets and at the dinner table. Election Day came and went. Lincoln didn't get a single vote in the South but won the election anyway by winning the popular vote in all but one of the northern states. White folks in the South were spittin' mad; so riled up that seven southern states quit the Union, followed by four others not long after. The states formed their own country, the Confederate States of America, and elected Jefferson Davis their president. President Lincoln demanded they stop all of the foolishness and come back to the Union, but they didn't pay him any mind. The South was fixin' for a fight. And so Lincoln had to give 'em one.

Harriet Tubman

4

LINCOLN'S WAR

"Surely 'war is hell'—but slavery is worse."
—Nat Love, former slave

The good Lord blessed the South with beautiful country. There are big green mountains and wide rivers full of jumpin' fish, and cypress swamps and forests with giant trees as tall as buildings, each full of squeakin' birds and critters. There are even white sand beaches with warm water and palm trees. Most important, the South is blessed with deep rich soil capable of raising crops of all kinds. It's the reason so many plantations were built down South. Larger plantations had beautiful gardens and big houses with rows of old oak trees draped with Spanish moss. They were filled with the finest things: grandfather clocks, velvet and silk couches, expensive rugs, and chandeliers of colored glass. Visitors to the property might have felt like they had just reached the gardens of heaven. That was until they caught sight of African men and women slaves whose raggedy clothes, sad faces, and smelly bodies revealed the ugly truth that this was no heaven at all. Those fancy homes came at the high price of blood and sweat of people who never knew liberty. The time would come when all of those white folks in the North and the South who benefited from slavery would pay dearly for the trouble it had started.

Pap's master's great mansion

That time came to pass in the spring of 1861. It was very tense after the South had left the Union. Most of the Union troops stationed in the South gave up their posts and went North—all but the ones who withdrew to Fort Sumter off the coast of South Carolina. Confederate "Rebel" troops surrounded them and cut off all their supplies. Finally, early one morning it reached the boiling point. The Rebels fired first and showered the fort with cannonballs until the next day. Surprisingly, no one was killed, but the fort took a beating and the Union troops surrendered. It was the start of the Civil War.

Pap was a young man when the war began. When the line was drawn between the Union and the Confederacy, some southern families who lived in border states had to choose sides. Rather than stay in the Union, a handful of slave owners abandoned their plantations and sent their slaves south into the Confederacy. When Maryland sided with the Union, slaves on Pap's plantation were split between the master's two older sons in Virginia. Pap and some thirty other slaves were sent to a plantation in Richmond owned by the master's eldest son. A few months after they had settled there, Pap was out in the cotton fields when he heard a loud boom. Sounded like thunder, only there weren't any rain clouds. He heard it again, and all of the slaves were frightened. The overseer said it was the sound of cannons. "Just over that hill, the Rebels are killin' the Yankees for trying to steal our property," he said. "They gon' kill you too if they catch you." Pap wondered just what property the overseer was talking about—ol' overseer didn't own a thing. Pretty soon they all got used to the sound of the cannons.

There was fighting all over the place. Slaves kept quiet around white folks but gossiped amongst each other about how Abe Lincoln was going to free the slaves. Pap couldn't wait on Uncle Abe, though. When the fighting came close enough, he upped and ran to the Yankee lines. Turned out they didn't kill him like the overseer had said they would, but they had him working hard as the devil, digging ditches and clearing dead and wounded soldiers from the battlefield; and he didn't eat as well as he had on the plantation. But he didn't care. He was free! And would you believe that the Missus had the nerve to be heartbroken when he ran away? Other slaves who made it to the Yankee lines told Pap she said he "deserted" them. Chile, please! You can't blame a person for taking his freedom when he gets the chance.

Pap said the battlefields were terrible, noisy places—one steady roar of guns and cannons. The windows

Pap as a Union soldier, 1863

Fort Wagner, South Carolina, 1863

in towns nearby were all broken from the shaking of the cannon blasts. On the ground, men were scattered round everywhere dead or wounded, some cussin' and some prayin'. Some moanin', and crying for water and great God a-mighty.

Black folks weren't allowed to fight in the early part of the war, only bury dead soldiers or build army camps. But they longed to be in the fight more than anything. They knew that if the South had its way, there'd be slaves from Canada to Florida. Frederick Douglass published antislavery appeals to the president in his newspaper and even met with him in person to convince him that it was time to put black folks in the war. Lincoln wasn't so sure about it. And he was slow, honey, slow as molasses to make up his mind. It took some doing, but in July of 1862 he finally agreed and allowed black folks in the army, although they had to wait until the year was out to join the blacks-only regiments, and were paid less than white soldiers. Pap got his chance to fight, too, and joined those boys who tried to take Fort Wagner in South Carolina. The good Lord must have been with him 'cause somehow he got through the battle without a scrape. The army was good for putting black soldiers in all kinds of dangerous situations that they had no business being in. But they fought anyway and earned the respect of their fellow soldiers. Black folks everywhere were proud of them.

Not long after that Lincoln set the slaves free. Well, most of them. He had heard that slaves were forced to help the South stay in the war by building their camps and digging trenches. If Lincoln freed the slaves, he would force the Rebels to have to do all that work themselves and cripple their numbers on the battle-field. So he set free all of the slaves in Rebel states by issuing his Emancipation Proclamation even though the Confederacy didn't recognize the power of the president of the Union. (The Proclamation didn't apply to some border states, though, because they weren't part of the Confederacy.) So to sweeten the pot Lincoln promised freedom to slaves in the Rebel states who fought in the Union army. And, honey, when the slaves heard that freedom part, heaps of them ran off to the Union, *especially* the ones in the border states.

Lincoln gave the Rebel states 'til the end of the year to surrender and rejoin the Union. None of them did though. So on the first day of January of 1863, all of the slaves were set free! Lord have mercy and hallelujah! It was a day that many folks thought would *never* come.

Abraham Lincoln

The war was over about two years later. The papers said that black soldiers made all the difference in the war, helping finish off the Rebels about a year early. Pap returned to his old plantation with two white soldiers to tell all the slaves that they were free. "Mens and womens," he told them, "you are today as free as white folks. You are free to do as you like 'cause Abraham Lincoln done decreed that you are." Pap saw his old master standing on the porch lookin' mighty sad. He went over to him and said in a very low voice, "Bottom rail on top now, suh."

There was a lot of excitement among the slaves. They was rejoicin' and singin'. They danced and had a big jamboree! Some of them looked puzzled, not sure what to do. Some folks upped and left right away, wandering between plantations looking for lost relatives and loved ones. Most folks stayed put until they could figure out what to do with their newfound freedom.

Just like that, four million Negro slaves were set free. Black folks were thankful to the heavens and to Abe Lincoln for having the courage to do what he felt was the right thing. The jamboree didn't last long though. Lincoln was shot dead a few days after Confederate General Robert E. Lee surrendered. Lincoln's vice president, Andrew Johnson, became president, and we quickly learned that he was no friend to black folks.

Freedom quilt

5

RECONSTRUCTION

"All men are created equal, says the great Declaration,
and now a great act attests this verity."
— Charles Sumner, U.S. senator, Massachusetts

When the slaves were set free, they didn't have nothin', and the ol' masters didn't give 'em nothin'. All of those folks had a mighty hard time. They had to start from scratch. In slavery time it was against the law for most black folks to own property, to vote, or to read. All of a sudden we had to find a way to make it on our own.

A few politicians had the "bright idea" that black people should be sent back to Africa—all four million of us. President Lincoln even seriously considered the idea before the end of the war. Even though some black folks made the trip, there was no way the government would pay to send all of those people back across the ocean. Besides, we didn't know Africa any more than we knew the south of France. We were born and raised in America, we were Americans by right, and America is where we would stay.

Southern white folks had to start over, too. Much of the South was destroyed by the war. Cities like Richmond and Atlanta were burned, abandoned, and looted by the soldiers. The great wealth of the proud South was gone. Deserted southern properties were given away, and the Confederate dollar wasn't worth a cup of

A young woman teaches her father how to read.

Freedmen

red Georgia clay. Young folks used to dig that money out of the garbage and play with it.

To help southerners and freed slaves get on their feet, the government planned to rebuild the South with a series of acts called Reconstruction. The Freedmen's Bureau, which oversaw Reconstruction efforts, gave a few former slaves each about forty acres of deserted land to cultivate and live on. Problem was, no one told the freedmen that the land was already owned by someone else. When the true owners of the land came back after the war, President Johnson ordered the freed slaves to give the land back.

Some black folks moved west to claim land and start over, or up North to work in cities. Most stayed and, like Pap, went to work for their old masters as sharecroppers. Sharecropping was an arrangement where workers would split the profit of a crop with the owner of the land. Ol' master paid for the seed, supplies, equipment, and living expenses and told Pap he had to pay him back for his share of the expenses at the end of the year. After Pap settled his debt to the owner, he'd get the rest of the money owed him for the crop. It sounded like a fair deal, but ol' master was a crook. When he and Pap settled at the end of the year, he always found a way *not* to pay Pap. He subtracted the cost of the seed, food, housing, and such from what he owed Pap, padding it here and there, figuring and figuring until it ended up with Pap owing *him*! Even if he wanted to, Pap couldn't say a word. The unwritten (but well-understood) rule was, *Never* contradict a white person, no matter what. That was reason enough to find yourself strung up from a tree. The best Pap could do was to try and make it back the next year, but he never did, honey. Sharecropping was a sneaky way of keeping black folks in the fields without having to pay them. Wasn't much different from slavery.

With the end of slavery, millions of former slaves finally had the right to learn to read, write, and figure. The Freedmen's Bureau helped set up and oversee free public schools and colleges all around the South. Scores of northern teachers flooded down to teach all the newly freed slaves and poor white folks who weren't able to go to school before the war. Black men also gained the right to vote, and with it they put some of our own folks in office; even sent a few to the House of Representatives.

These were very big steps, but our "progress" didn't come without a price. The time after the war was terrible for black folks. Even though we could vote and go to school, most of us were very poor and illiterate. Union soldiers occupied southern towns to keep the peace but didn't do much to protect black people from

Pap sharecropping

new groups of mean whites, like the Ku Klux Klan, who threatened us all year long. To stop black folks from voting, Klansmen marched in front of their homes wearing white sheets over their heads, shooting out the windows and burning homes to the ground, or worse, dragging black folks out of their homes to lynch them. The law didn't do a thing to stop it. Shoot, some of the men wearing the sheets *were* lawmen. It was their way of keeping us "in our place," wherever that was supposed to be. They couldn't stand to see us trying to be equal to whites. They were convinced that they were somehow superior to black people. My grandmother used to call it "the Sickness." Whatever it was, it was just plain mean, honey. Lord knows how those folks could fix it in their minds to do the things they did to us back then. It's a miracle we made it through.

After a while the government seemed to just give up on Reconstruction. Federal troops were sent back home and state governments wrote new laws called Jim Crow laws that divided everything by race: restaurants, libraries, theaters, schools, markets, drinking fountains, you name it. There were now two Americas—one white and one black—and the South slowly fell backward into something that looked a lot like slavery. Sharecroppers were stuck in the fields in debt to landowners; black people lived in fear of violence; and the vote was pushed out of reach with poll taxes, which people had to pay in order to vote and which were too high for most black folks. New laws like the grandfather clause said only people whose grandfathers had voted in prior elections could vote, which obviously made it impossible for black folks to vote. The North had won the Civil War; but the South, it won Reconstruction.

The burning cross was a warning to black folks, meant to keep them "in their place."

6

COWBOYS AND INDIANS: NATIVE AMERICANS AND WESTWARD NEGROES

"And to that Territory should such freemen go."
—Frederick Douglass

Black folks often talk about having a little Indian blood in the family, and it's hard to know if they are always being truthful. Maybe it makes them feel exotic or different from most black folks in some way. Or maybe it makes them feel more American. Who knows, honey? But it certainly *is* true in my family. When my granddaddy took his freedom, he was a young man. After the war, he was stationed out in Oklahoma with the 10th Cavalry, a unit of black soldiers the army had assembled out West to build forts, lay telegraph wire, and keep the peace among the locals and the Indian folk. They also built roads, protected stagecoaches and mail carriers, and mapped out uncharted western regions. The Choctaw Indians, who fought against the black soldiers, said their curly hair looked like the buffalo fur coats the soldiers wore and called them "Buffalo Soldiers." The white soldiers and townsfolk didn't always give them the credit they deserved at first, but their minds were soon changed after seeing how bravely they fought in the Plains

Pap and Aunt Sarah

Indian Wars. The Buffalo Soldiers won the respect of both their peers *and* their enemies.

It was in Oklahoma where he met and married my grandmother, a Seminole Indian we called Aunt Sarah. Aunt Sarah was very short, had smooth brown skin, and was about as chatty as an oak tree. But sometimes she spoke about her people. Before the war, the Seminoles, who lived in the northern part of Florida, took in runaway slaves in exchange for their labor. Black folks who lived with them became part of the tribe, often intermarried, and even became tribal leaders. The government and slave owners who lived close enough to the Florida border wanted to stop this kind of thing because it was a threat to slavery, putting ideas in the heads of slaves who were looking for a better way of life. In the 1830s and '40s, the government spent millions of dollars and lost thousands of soldiers fighting with the Seminoles, trying to push them off their land. Eventually, though, most of the Seminoles were forced to leave Florida for the West, but hundreds of them moved farther south into the swamplands and stood their ground. Other Indian tribes like the Cherokee, Creek, and Choctaw didn't fare as well. About one hundred thousand Indians were either swindled out of their lands by treaties the government didn't honor or made to leave at gunpoint and marched hundreds of miles to live out in the middle of Oklahoma.

In 1862 the government passed the Homestead Act to encourage people to move west. They had already pushed out most of the Indians and put them on reservations, making way for new railway lines and thousands of white folks who were looking for a new life or fortunes in gold in the West. Black folks went too.

Frederick Douglass urged freed slaves to move west as a way to stake a claim in the growing country. Thousands of freed slaves traveled west by wagon or mule and found life there to be a little kinder than in the South, but only a little. It was by no means an easy life. There had been a lot of fighting over slavery out in Oklahoma and Nebraska, so when black folks showed up looking to claim land, you can imagine they weren't exactly greeted with a welcome mat. They were barred from going to public schools and not allowed to vote or buy land, and in some places they tried to stop black folks from settling there altogether by changing the law—made them pay a steep fine for entering the state and even forced some of them to leave at gunpoint. If black folks couldn't settle in a white town, they found a place where they could or found some land and built their own town. There were several all-black towns in states like Oklahoma, with black

Schoolteacher, Nicodemus, Kansas

schools and shops, with black doctors, clerks, sheriffs, and such—they even had black cowboys like Nat Love, whose adventures made for good reading, and Bill Pickett, who became a great rodeo performer.

Life on the frontier was rough. In most parts there weren't any trees, so folks had to build their homes out of mud bricks and cow pies. For fresh water they had to dig wells. They grew their vegetables and hunted for food. Every day on those flat prairies was a fight to survive, but fighting to live as a free person out there was always better than living under the whip on a southern plantation.

My grandmother on my mother's side was from Tennessee. There were six children in her family all together: four boys and two girls. After the war her older sister, my aunt Mary, moved out to Montana to work with the nuns. She was as big and strong as a man, and acted like one too. She smoked, drank, chopped wood, and drove a wagon for the nuns and the post office. I even heard she knocked a white man out cold in broad daylight for not paying his laundry bill. They'd hang you down South for something like that, honey. But the locals didn't bother her. She lived to be eighty years old.

Plenty of black folks like Pap and Aunt Mary found a measure of freedom out West, but when Pap's time in the service was over, he and Aunt Sarah moved back to Virginia to live with us. He was glad to be with his family again, but Pap found that he hadn't missed Jim Crow one bit. Abraham Lincoln said once that if some of us can enjoy the fruits of freedom while our brothers and sisters are still bound by their countrymen, then none of us are truly free. At the end of the century, most black folks were still trapped in the South. And it would take something drastic to get us to leave.

Pap as a Buffalo Soldier

7

TURN OF THE CENTURY AND THE GREAT MIGRATION

"Freedom could make folks proud, but it didn't make 'em rich."

—Felix Haywood, former slave

The years after Reconstruction were some of the darkest since slavery. After we had made some progress, the rug was pulled out from under us and control of the South ended up back in the hands of the same breed of people who had always had it. We were expected to keep quiet, walk with our eyes downcast, and bow to white folks, being ever so careful not to cause trouble. It was a dangerous time for us. We were being kidnapped, lynched, shot, and burned all over the South. We had to stick together and watch out for each other, like a big family. Millions of black folks were trapped in the South under the thumb of Jim Crow, and we might have stayed that way a lot longer if it weren't for all of the trouble in Europe.

Now, it's not particularly easy to describe what was happening in Europe at the time, but I can tell you that in 1914, Archduke Ferdinand (who was next in line to the throne of the Austro-Hungarian empire) was assassinated. In a very short time, countries all over Europe started choosing sides, lining up for war. Before we knew it, countries all around the world were pulled into their mess, ours included. With a war coming,

Southern family migrating north, circa 1940

America needed to build weapons. There were plenty of factories up North that, at the time, were filled with European immigrant workers (women and black folks were generally not welcome), but many more people were needed to build weapons for the coming war.

But as fighting began in Europe, America stopped letting most of the immigrants into the country. With so many new factories, there weren't enough immigrants to take those jobs, so as a last resort, the factory owners gave the jobs to women and black folks.

Word about the new jobs spread like wildfire. The *Chicago Defender*, a black newspaper that was passed around in churches and barbershops, invited "all to come North." On railroad trains porters bragged about how well black folks were doing up North. Family members who had already gone there wrote letters saying that they earned several times more than what they had on the farm and that black folks could vote, go to good schools and fancy movie theaters, and dress like movie stars. It all sounded pretty fine. Despite the trouble we had with white folks and the boll weevil beetle that was eatin' up the cotton and destroying farmers' crops, most of us had grown to love the South and never seriously thought about leaving. The South was home. But like hundreds of thousands of black folks who weighed the trouble of living there against the opportunities up North, we felt it was time to go.

Now, leaving was easier said than done. White folks didn't exactly want us to go. After all, *we* worked their fields and paid their rents. If we all upped and left, they would have been in a real fix. So they tried their best to stop us. They banned Northern black papers; police officers harassed black folks at the train stations; clerks ignored us when we tried to buy train tickets; and they even stopped the train service in some places altogether. But it didn't work, honey. No matter what they did, they couldn't stop us from leaving any more than they could stop the rain from falling. We had made up our minds.

My family went by train like most black folks, but some drove, rode on horseback or on a mule, or even walked. It took almost a full day to ride by train from Virginia to Chicago. We celebrated when we made it across the Mason-Dixon Line and moved from the Jim Crow car to cars where white folks sat. Some people even started praying and singing. The train was full of black folks on their way to Chicago, Philadelphia,

New arrivals, Chicago, circa 1915

Pittsburgh, Detroit, or New York City. We learned that southern black folks were pouring into neighborhoods like Harlem and the South Side of Chicago bringing southern comforts like jazz and blues music and southern cooking to the big cities.

When we moved north, we had to change our way of doing things. In the South we mostly depended on the owner of the land for what we needed: food, shelter, schools (raggedy as they were), and work. Everything was purchased on credit. But up North we had to find it all for ourselves. It made us much more independent.

In many ways life was better for us. Pap, Daddy, Mother, and all of the grown folks in my family found plenty of work, and we felt we had a bit more freedom; but we also learned that Jim Crow had made the trip right along with us. There was only one part of town where we could find a place to live, and the best jobs were closed to us. We also didn't know that we had all walked right into the middle of what would be a huge fight. Owners of the factories were making more money than they could count, while everybody else made pennies on the dollar, working long hours in unsafe factories; and it made a lot of people angry.

Workers formed labor unions and organized strikes on the railroads, in mills, coal mines, shipping docks. Seemed like everybody was ready to strike—everybody but black folks. When we tried it, the factory owners just ignored us. Only the porters made any headway some years later. The owners fought dirty, too, honey. When white folks picketed, the owners knew black workers weren't allowed into many of the unions, so they brought them into the factories to break the strike. It made for some real problems between black and white folks up North—and for very dangerous times. There were race riots and lynchings all over the North and South because of it.

Like most black folks, Booker T. Washington, our most popular leader in the early 1900s, wanted equal treatment. He felt the best way to get it was for us to stop all the fussin' and get to work. In the years after Reconstruction he built Tuskegee Institute into a great school that taught black folks skills they could use to get ahead. Booker T. thought we could gain respect by providing services to white folks and by showing that we could make our own money. White folks loved the idea, of course, but many black folks disagreed with him. The problem was bigger than money. Racism had been spoon-fed to generations of American children

War munitions factory, circa 1914

UNITED OFFICE
and PROFESSIONAL
WORKERS-CIO
ON STRIKE
UNITED OFFICE
and PROFESSIONAL
WORKERS-CIO
ON STRIKE
MID CITY REALTY
UNFAIR
MID CITY REALTY
UNFAIR
YET
Strikers

MID CITY REALTY
UNFAIR
MID CITY REALTY
UNFAIR
WHY PAY RENT
WHEN your BUILDING
SLAVERY
was abolished

for hundreds of years, and it had convinced many black and white folks that white people were better than black people in every way. The hatred it stirred between the two races took on a life of its own. America badly needed to find a way to get past it.

In any case, the fight for equality was put on hold when America entered the First World War in the middle of April 1917. Black men were eager to join the military, although very few black troops saw combat. Most black soldiers worked in labor battalions. The war ended about a year later in 1918.

It's funny how things work out sometimes. War is a terrible thing, but strangely enough this one did black folks some good. It had pulled over a million of us out of the South and helped us onto our feet.

Booker T. Washington

8

HARLEM AND THE VOTE FOR WOMEN

"We return from fighting. We return fighting."
—W.E.B. DuBois, scholar, PhD

"The right to vote is ours. Have it we must. Use it we will."
—Elizabeth Cady Stanton, women's suffragist

The summer before the war officially ended was dreadful. It was hot, people were hungry, streets were crowded because there wasn't enough work or housing, the soldiers were coming home from the war, and southerners kept coming North, adding to the crowds. The combination seemed to make *some* white folks lose their good minds. Mobs of angry whites stormed into black neighborhoods and grabbed people off the street and beat them to death. All summer long they were burning black folks' homes and businesses in big cities all over the country to try to scare us away.

But this generation of black folks was different from past generations. Many of our parents and grandparents had often looked for help from good white folks in hard times like these. But *this* generation had grown

Black neighborhoods were burned and looted all over the country.

up and into its own. Many of them had graduated from public schools or black universities like Howard and Tuskegee, and education had given them the tools they needed to move forward. We all felt like we were on a mission to "uplift the race" and do away with that feeling of being less than white folks. This time we looked no farther than our front doorstep for help. It was like the souls of black folks all over the North were waking up.

Now, Chicago was something special. We had the strip on the South Side where we could go watch a movie, see a show, or have soul food that was so good you wanted to go and slap the cook. Our Negro League baseball team, the Chicago American Giants, was the best in town; but at that particular time, most of the action was in Harlem, in New York City. Folks would come visit from there looking sharp as a tack, honey. They brought with them fancy clothes and the best jazz records. Jazz was a new kind of music where horn players, drummers, and piano players made up beautiful music right on the spot! The music would swing and sway back and forth, making us dizzy with the sounds of Jelly Roll Morton, Ella Fitzgerald, Duke Ellington . . . oh, they just put a spell on us. Jazz music took over the country. More jazz records sold than any other kind of music, and all the young folks couldn't get enough of it. Everybody seemed to want to learn to play an instrument and be in a jazz band.

On the weekend we would paint the town red, honey, dancing all night at the Savoy in Chicago, wearing holes in the floor. Folks talked about Josephine Baker, who danced in the Cotton Club and became a big star in Europe, and artists Aaron Douglass and Archibald Motley, who painted big pictures of black folks, strong and proud, just the way we liked to see ourselves. We read black writers from Harlem, like Langston Hughes, Zora Neale Hurston, and James Weldon Johnson, who told our stories with beauty and style. For the first time ever black folks were in the limelight, and the whole world was watching. The "New Negroes," as author Alain Locke called us, had arrived, and we were beautiful.

Black folks were as busy as a swarm of honeybees uptown in Harlem, and downtown was abuzz too. Women had decided to step out of the kitchen to get the vote and were marching up and down the streets of New York City and Washington, DC, trying to get it. Since America was founded, women never had any say about

Harlem couple

Big band

what happened outside the home. We were expected to marry, have children, keep house, and obey our husbands. In fact, at that time women really weren't much more than property—barely a step above being a slave. We were not allowed to own property if we were married, not allowed to attend college, not allowed any respectable career outside of teaching or nursing—and, of course, we were not allowed to vote. It wasn't fair. Half of the people in America were women, and yet we weren't allowed a say about how the country was being run. It was very much a man's world, and we were tired of it.

Women had been fighting to get the vote since before the Civil War. Over tea and biscuits and at church rallies, old ladies and young women, black and white, wrote passionate letters to politicians and published articles in newspapers, pleading their case for the vote. They even wrote a Declaration of Rights and Sentiments that read "We hold these truths to be self-evident that all men *and women* are created equal."

In the spring of 1912 women took to Washington, DC, and New York City streets and marched for our right to vote. Black women like Ida B. Wells marched with them the following year, even though white women didn't want us there and made us march in the back. And the men, they tried their best to stop the march. Crowds of them gathered along the sidewalk yelling things like "Go back to the kitchen!" and throwing trash at us. It was really something to see all of those boys treat us that way. Especially since it was we, black women, who had raised so many of them. We had raised many of their parents and grandparents, too! Honey, it broke our hearts, but we just walked right past them. We were *not* going back to the kitchen. Instead, on the second day of November, 1920, we marched our legs right into the voting booth, because we'd finally won the right to vote. Well . . . it was really only northern women who got the vote. The law allowed southern women to vote, but the truth was that southern men made it very hard for women to exercise the right at the polls.

Our progress was right in step with what was happening up North. People were happy because they were working and making a little money, and there were plenty of new things to buy, like automobiles and telephones. It seems like the good times would go on forever, but there was a big storm comin', honey. And soon people everywhere would be in serious trouble.

Black women's suffrage

9

HARD TIMES AND WORLD WAR II

"I learned that I was in two wars, one against the foreign enemy, the other against prejudice at home." —Jackie Robinson

"I love my America. And let somebody tell me it isnt mine." —E. G. McConnell, private, Company 76-1st Tank Battalion

My uncle Jesse had a farm down in Alabama with horses, cows, and chickens. He raised cotton and peanuts, and also had a little patch of fruit and vegetables. Uncle Jesse and his family had made a good life for themselves out there in the country. Most of his neighbors were white folks, but there were a few black farmers sprinkled about. He often had trouble with his white neighbors because they considered him competition. In the South, black folks had to be careful about doing too well. If they raised a better crop than their white neighbors, their crops and mills could end up in flames.

For a spell there were quite a few black planters in the South, but that changed when the boll weevils

Out of work

came back. Folks like Uncle Jesse had to switch crops or move away to start over. Southerners still depended on the cotton industry, so they had some real hard times when the planters left. Most northerners worked in factories, earning much more than southerners who still mostly lived in the countryside and worked on farms. Very soon things got even harder.

On Thursday, October 24, 1929, the U.S. stock market crashed. Only one day before, business was great, and stocks were traded at higher prices than they ever had been. But that Thursday, Americans could only watch as the market fell and stock brokers panicked, selling the same stocks for pennies on the dollar. Banks, mines, and other businesses went bankrupt. Soon the country was plunged into a very bad economic time called the Great Depression. Millions of people lost every nickel they kept in the banks, and many more lost their jobs and then their homes. Black folks were hit especially hard. Many were thrown off the land they worked and were forced to live in poverty. Some southerners were able to keep their jobs because the cost of labor was much less than up North, but their pay fell so low, it wasn't enough to live on. Millions of people were scared and hungry. Everywhere there were long food lines, and people in New York who lost their homes set up tents in city parks. To make things worse, there was a drought in the Midwest. Crops dried up, and farmers were forced to abandon their land. People looked for help from the government, but the folks on Capitol Hill couldn't do much.

The hard times lasted for about ten years. All the while Adolf Hitler, the new leader of Germany who had come to power in 1933, started making trouble in Europe. It was only the beginning of something bigger than anyone could have ever imagined.

In the late thirties a young black boxer by the name of Joe Louis fought a German fighter named Max Schmeling. Hitler bragged that Schmeling was going to show the world how Germans were a "supreme race" by winning the fight. Hitler didn't care much for black folks, or anyone else who wasn't blond and blue-eyed. Louis had lost to that young man two years before and hoped to fix things on this go round. It grew into a really big thing—something closer to a huge political event rather than a boxing match. The eyes of the whole world were fixed on those two young men. When the bell rang, Louis jumped out of his corner and

Heavyweight boxer Joe Louis Barrow

beat that poor fellow into a pulp in a single round! So much for "supreme," honey. We celebrated, but deep down we all knew that it was just a boxing match. The real fight was much worse.

We followed what was happening in Europe, listening to the radio and reading the papers. It was such a frightful thing. The Nazis had it in their minds to take over the whole world. They had taken over Germany by assassinating political leaders and then began invading neighboring countries. By the middle of 1941, the Nazis had occupied much of Europe. And even worse, there were rumors that they were murdering the Jewish people by the thousands—shooting, starving, gassing, and burning those poor people to death.

America tried hard to stay out of it, but then on Sunday, December 7, 1941, Japanese planes flew over to Hawaii and bombed our naval base at Pearl Harbor, killing thousands of our servicemen in a surprise attack. We couldn't stay out of it anymore, honey. It was time to saddle up and fight. The next day, President Franklin Roosevelt declared war on Japan, and every person in America was behind him.

Young men and women from every state signed up to serve in the war, and many more were drafted. Lord knows I couldn't go as I had to take care of my own children, but my two younger brothers went off to that war. Not that I wanted them to go, mind you. It was the hardest thing in the world, but I understood why they wanted to go and what they'd be fighting for. So we gave them our blessing and prayed we'd live to see them come home.

There were some white folks who thought this was a white man's war and turned black folks away when they went to sign up. But we had just as much to lose as they did. Maybe even more, considering the Nazis' feelings about us. Some black folks thought that the worst place in the world for a young black man was in the United States Army. And they were right, to a point. Black soldiers were at the mercy of their white superiors, some of whom were southerners who didn't like black folks. They were segregated from white soldiers and sent to the front in battle or made to swab the decks, cook, clean, and unload weapons from ships. That wasn't the "service" they signed up for. Some black soldiers didn't mind it, but a lot of those young men signed up to fight, not to serve or clean up after white folks.

White officers believed that black men weren't smart or brave enough to fight with white soldiers, or fly

My youngest brother, Joshua, a Tuskegee pilot

planes, or drive tanks. But after we invaded Europe in the summer of 1944, the first lady, Eleanor Roosevelt, pushed President Roosevelt to put black soldiers in the fight. She had a good heart and was a great friend to black folks, and anyone who was in need.

The military gave in, calling it an "experiment." The Tuskegee Airmen (the 332nd) and the 761st Tank Battalion were put into action. Now, I'm not bragging (much), but our boys were some of the best combat soldiers and bomber escorts in the world. The 332nd pilots had the record for losing the fewest bomber planes in more than two hundred missions and were so good at escorting and protecting them, they were specially requested for the job.

When most tank battalions lasted only seventeen days on the battlefield, the 761st, an all-black unit, fought for one hundred eighty-three days straight, longer than any other battalion in the whole war. They helped win the Battle of the Bulge. And I'm proud to say that both of my brothers were right there with them, giving it to the Germans. But would you believe that after all the fighting they did for the country, the black soldiers were mostly ignored? White units got their medals during the war and were even commended by the president while our soldiers weren't honored until several decades later.

It didn't make sense. We had gone to war for our country to stop racist people from taking over the world, and yet at home Jim Crow held us in his grip just as tightly as before. When the war was over, both of my brothers returned and saw that nothing had changed. They had been to places like France and England, where black folks were treated just the same as white folks, and came home only to have to sit in the back of the bus. We figured, if our soldiers were able to fight and defeat racism overseas, why couldn't *we* do it here? Their stories about equality in Europe let us know that this kind of thing was possible. It weighed heavy on our minds and pushed many of us to stand up again to fight for what we deserved. It was time to make things right. Jim Crow's days were numbered.

My younger brother James, with the 761st Tank Battalion, Germany, circa 1944

10

BLACK INNOVATION

"Education is the key to unlock the golden door of freedom."
—George Washington Carver, inventor

*Y*ou may have heard folks say that black people invented shoes. But, chile, that is *not* true. Everybody invented shoes. But it *is* true that in the 1880s a black man named Ernst Matzeliger invented a machine that made the *process* of making shoes a lot cheaper and faster. Matzeliger is one of many black folks whose ideas have made the lives of everyone in the world a lot better.

Black people have been making inventions since slavery days, plenty of very practical things that helped us do the work we were forced to do. Africans invented new ways of fishing, farming, basket weaving, ironsmithing. Since then, we've invented ways of keeping food fresh with curing salts and refrigeration, lubricating engines, safely linking train cars, controlling traffic flow, improving lighting fixtures, helping firefighters breathe in smoke-filled rooms, and making supercomputers faster, among many other things.

Everybody knows that we have created brilliant types of music like spirituals, jazz, blues, gospel, rock and roll, and so on. And that we have done very well in athletics. Yes, honey, we all know that, even if we try to downplay it. But we've done so much more. Have you ever used an ironing board? Sat in a folding chair?

African American inventors and inventions

Used a dustpan? Ridden in a convertible or on a horse saddle? Read an almanac? Used a fountain pen that did not require dipping it into an inkwell? Sat at a traffic light? Seen a gas mask? Used a golf tee? Turned on an electric lightbulb? Eaten food delivered by a truck? Used an ice-cream scooper? Gone to a blood bank? Used a batting helmet or shin guards, or enjoyed potato chips? I'll bet you have. Most people don't know that all of these things were invented by or improved by black folks.

One of our finest inventors was a fellow named Elijah McCoy. Among many other useful things, like the ironing board and lawn sprinkler, he invented a lubricating cup that oiled the gears of a train engine. Several people tried to copy his invention, but folks who knew quality only wanted the "real McCoy." Another inventor, Lewis Latimer, improved on Edison's electric lamp by inventing a filament that could be produced much more cheaply. George Washington Carver was one our most gifted inventors. He loved nature; and outside of his genius for making plants grow, he invented hundreds of products from soybeans, sweet potatoes, and peanuts—from soap, to ink, to synthetic rubber. Frederick M. Jones invented a portable X-ray machine and a refrigeration unit for food delivery trucks, ships, and airplanes. Dr. Charles Drew figured out how to separate blood cells from plasma to preserve blood longer than the week or so it lasted when it was whole, which led to the creation of blood banks all over the world. Annie Malone and Madam C. J. Walker invented hair-growing lotions that were so popular, they made millions of dollars. Walker used her wealth to help with the movement to get the vote for women. Garrett Morgan invented the first automatic traffic signal. Granville Woods invented a train-to-train communication system. Otis Boykin invented a control device for guided missiles and computers, and the pacemaker . . . etcetera, etcetera.

I could go on forever, honey, but I've left out what is probably the most important idea ever introduced to America by an African American. It was brought to us by a young preacher from Georgia who used it to change the course of history. It was a tactic that he learned from Mahatma Gandhi, who used it to free his people in India from British rule. The young preacher combined it with ideas from the Good Book and America's Declaration of Independence to create a new message that spoke to all people, a message that had more power than any fist, gun, or bomb.

This young man was Dr. Martin Luther King Jr., and the idea was the peaceful protest.

Dr. Martin Luther King Jr.

11

JIM CROW'S A-DYING

*"If America is to remain a first-class nation,
it can no longer have second-class citizens."*
—Dr. Martin Luther King Jr.

I heard a story once about a black boy in the South who used to ride the city bus home from school every day. As was the custom, he sat in the back of the bus just behind the sign that split the bus into "white" and "colored" sections. One afternoon a white kid got on the bus and sat right in front of the sign where the black boy was sitting. He stared at the young fellow and then at the sign, back and forth, for several stops, as if to taunt him. There was a door at the back of the bus; and when the bus pulled up to the next stop, the black boy grabbed the sign, stuck it in his satchel, and took off running down the street. The white kid yelled to the driver, "That boy stole the sign!" The driver jumped off the bus and yelled at him to come back, but the young fellow hightailed it all the way home. He still has that sign, too. Now, it was not right for him to break the law, but just like many people in the South who were tired of Jim Crow laws, he felt that if the law says that you are less than equal to whites, then it is a bad law. And some laws need to be broken.

Jackie Robinson, 1947

After World War II, a young soldier named Jackie Robinson joined the Negro League baseball team in Kansas City. He played well enough to catch the eye of Branch Rickey, a part owner of the Major League Brooklyn Dodgers. Rickey was so impressed with Robinson, he hired him to play for his team despite the ban on black players. Jackie became the first black ballplayer to play in the Major Leagues since the 1880s. White folks in the ballpark harassed that man for two years straight. White players pushed and spiked him, while white fans yelled and threatened him. But, in spite of it all, Jackie played very well. He went on to be one of the best players in baseball and showed people that black folks were more than equals on and off the field. It was the beginning of a new day for baseball, and for the country.

Now, I told you that our country grew big and strong from slave labor, but it came of age by way of the Second World War. America came out of World War II the strongest nation in the world, but in the South Jim Crow was still the law of the land. Laws were supposed to make black and white folks "separate but equal"; but black folks were only separate. While white folks generally had the best schools and supplies, black schools were shabby at best. They had very few buses that worked, black children were crowded into one-room schools, supplies were always short, books were outdated leftovers from white schools, and in some places high school wasn't even offered to black children because the local government felt that they didn't need it. Nothing about the school system was "equal." We knew that the key to giving our children a chance in life was a good education. And the only way they would get it was if we fought for it. So began the struggle for truly equal education.

Several southern black parents began trying to put their children in white public schools and were, of course, turned away. Reverend Brown from Kansas tried to send his little girl to the white school near their house in Topeka and was met with the same result—so he sued the school board. A lawyer with the NAACP, Thurgood Marshall, took up the case and argued it before the Supreme Court. He won, too! And black children gained the right to attend white public schools. It was hard for the children, though. They just wanted to go to good schools like everybody else, but the people down there were so mean about the whole thing. Integrating schools was very dangerous business, you know; but the children were brave. Every morning all year long the children had to face angry crowds of shouting and spitting parents, and were harassed by their

Brave children, Little Rock, Arkansas

classmates and teachers. In Little Rock, Arkansas, nine black students were blocked from entering their new high school. President Eisenhower had to send armed troops to escort the children into the building. In Birmingham, Alabama, a preacher tried to enroll his children in a white school, and he and his wife were beaten up very badly. A few years later the governor in Alabama himself stood in front of the door to a university to block black students from entering. What kind of grown man would do such a thing? It took a very long time to get the schools to abide by the Court's decision. Having the right to do something, and being allowed to do it, are two different things. One by one, segregated schools had to be sued to allow black children to enroll. And still, to this day the schools still aren't all the way integrated because of clever neighborhood zoning or lack of busing.

Busing was a problem in Alabama, too. In 1955, in Montgomery, a seamstress left work and headed home on a segregated bus late one afternoon. She took a seat at the front of the "colored" section of the bus. Now, if you can believe this, when a white fellow got on the bus, the driver told her to get up and give her seat to him. Excuse me? Mrs. Parks said no. The driver came back raising a fuss, talking about how she had better get up or he'd call the police to come and arrest her. Like every other black person in America, Mrs. Parks was tired. Tired of being treated like a second-class citizen. She was sick and tired of giving up her seat to white folks on buses; sick and tired of being refused service in restaurants, hospitals, department stores, and hotels and of having to buy second-rate food from the back doors of cafés and entering movie theaters from the rear to sit in hot balconies to see a show; sick and tired of being forced to drink from segregated water fountains when she shouldn't have to. Indeed, Mrs. Parks and millions more of us were "sick and tired of being sick and tired." Mrs. Parks did not move for that white man on the bus and was arrested and sent to jail.

Now, it could have ended there. When Mrs. Parks got out of jail she could have just gone back to work. You see, she was not the first black person in Montgomery to be arrested for refusing to give up a seat on a bus to a white person, but she was very well-known and respected in her community. She was a perfect example of the unfair treatment that black people were made to suffer in Montgomery, and the rest of the South for that matter. The community rallied around Mrs. Parks, and black leaders decided to organize a

Rosa Parks

boycott of the buses in Montgomery. They chose a young preacher from Atlanta named Dr. Martin Luther King Jr. to lead the boycott. It was agreed that no black person in Montgomery would ride a bus on the following Monday. And come Monday, every bus in Montgomery was just about as empty as a poor man's pockets, honey. Black folks boycotted the buses the next day, the next week, and the next month. Mostly black maids and washwomen rode the buses in Montgomery, and for months they walked to work or found rides with car pools, rain or shine. Without their business the bus companies almost went bankrupt. The boycott continued through the winter and into the next year. Of course, the businesses and government in Montgomery fought the boycott tooth and nail. Even bombed Dr. King's house. But in the end they had to surrender. Dr. King knew that if black folks held to the boycott and did not fight back with violence but with a *peaceful* protest, they would be victorious. And on December 20, 1956, three hundred and eighty-one days after the boycott began, Dr. King called for the end of the boycott after the Supreme Court ruled that black folks all over America had the right to sit anywhere they wanted on the buses. Without any shouting, shooting, fighting, or fussing, black folks won a major battle for equality through nonviolent demonstrations. Glory, hallelujah! Oh, how we celebrated all over the country! It was a sweet and wonderful victory. There would be setbacks and victories to come in the very near future, but we savored this one for quite some time, honey.

Bus boycott, Montgomery, Alabama, 1956

12
REVOLUTION

"We knew we were going to change the world."
—Angela Davis, revolutionary

Something good had started in Montgomery, and it spread all across the country. Young people grabbed hold of the movement the grown folks had started and took it over. To show how different they were from their parents' generation, they started wearing their hair long, and their clothes became louder and more colorful. And the music, honey, the music was even louder and more soulful. The sounds of angry electric guitars and powerful drums echoed through our neighborhoods as we sang along with James Brown, "Say it loud, I'm black and I'm proud!" and Sam Cooke, "A change is gonna come." College kids started to challenge the segregation laws, starting with the Woolworth's café in Greensboro, North Carolina. Four black students just went in there and sat down at the white folks' lunch counter. They were later put in jail, but people heard about it and started doing it all over the South, going into whites-only movie theaters, pools, churches, libraries, and such, trying to break Jim Crow. Dr. King joined them too, and there were even a number of us older folks who felt brave enough to get on board. We called ourselves Freedom Riders, and we filled cars and buses with white and black folks and rode all

Southern Woolworth's Café

over the South breaking the segregation laws. This was a very dangerous thing, mind you. Those of us who were lucky were merely arrested and put in jail for a few days; but many others were beaten very badly by policemen and mobs of white townsfolk, and their buses and cars were burned. Three years later, Ku Klux Klan members killed not only black folks, but some of the *white* folks who were helping organize the movement and get black folks registered to vote, and believe me when I tell you that it made *everybody* feel a little scared. But we kept moving forward. Like Dr. King told us, "We've come too far to turn back now."

There were other leaders in the movement, like A. Philip Randolph, Malcolm X, Adam Powell, Fannie Lou Hamer, and Medgar Evers; but it was Dr. King who spoke loudest of all. His message was clear: We cannot win this battle with violence. We cannot win it with hate. We can only win it with persistence, love, and nonviolence, and by reminding the nation and the people on Capitol Hill that our forefathers made a promise of freedom and justice for all when they signed that paper. We would become the nation's moral conscience and fight the battle for justice and equality.

Dr. King marched us all over the South trying to get the attention of the whole country. We just loved him and would have followed him anywhere. When he spoke, his powerful voice gave you *chills*. It shook your spirit and got you excited, and calmed you when you were scared. He was patient and took time to listen to everybody, even the children. And he was handsome, too, honey, which didn't hurt one bit.

In May of 1963, Dr. King and his team went down to Birmingham, Alabama, the most dangerous place in the South for black folks. They went to work marching people all over the city and got everybody's attention when they marched six hundred children through Kelly Ingram Park. Most were teenagers, but some were as young as six years old. They skipped school to march on downtown Birmingham, holding hands and singing. Policemen ordered them to stop and then sicced their dogs on them and sprayed them with fire hoses. That water was strong enough to knock the bark off of a tree, and they turned it on the children. It knocked them down and ripped their shirts off; even pinned them up against buildings and trees. It was downright shameful. Pictures of the march were shown on television screens and in newspapers all over the world. President John F. Kennedy had no choice but to settle things in Birmingham.

Later that summer, Dr. King, Dr. Philip Randolph, and several leaders in the movement invited people

Kelly Ingram Park, Birmingham, Alabama, 1963

from all over the country to join them in Washington, DC, for a peaceful demonstration on the Mall to try and pass a civil rights bill to promote civil rights and economic equality for black people. Just about everybody I knew made the trip. We rode on a bus for hundreds of miles all the way to Washington. It was such a glorious day. We filed off the bus and joined a parade of people who were marching and singing, headed for the Lincoln Memorial, where great crowds of people were crammed together on the Mall. Black, white, brown, red, and yellow folks were everywhere; it seemed like the whole *world* had come. It was almost like a dream. Seeing so many people there made us realize we were not alone in this struggle for equality.

There were several speakers throughout the afternoon, but what I remember most is when Dr. King spoke. His powerful voice rose and fell and echoed over a sea of people as he spoke about his dream for America. He shouted, "I have a dream that my four little children will one day live in a nation where they will not be judged by the color of their skin, but by the content of their character. . . . And if America is to be a great nation, this must become true. . . . Free at last! Free at last! Thank God Almighty, we are free at last!" Dr. King roared. By the time he finished, people on the Mall were hugging and shouting, and swaying and crying. It was a magnificent speech. It felt like we all got a little church on that Wednesday afternoon.

It wasn't long before President Kennedy promised to send a civil rights bill to Congress to guarantee equal rights to all American citizens, no matter what their color. He never got a chance to see it through, though. Just a few months later, he was shot and killed on a visit to Texas.

President Lyndon Johnson signed the Civil Rights Act into law in 1964 and the Voting Rights Act the following year. The government had finally said to the world that Jim Crow was dead. The time had come at last when the words written by our forefathers—"that all men are created equal"—were honored by our government. It had taken hundreds of years, millions of lives, marches, martyrs, protests, wars, and much more for America to come closer than ever before to becoming what it was meant to be. Lord knows there were plenty more battles to fight, many more struggles and troubles to overcome; but at last the idea that everybody counts was within reach. It was a glorious victory for all Americans. and the beginning of a new struggle for every American to ensure that we "hold these truths to be self evident, that all men (and women) are created equal."

March on Washington, DC, 1963

Dr. Martin Luther King Jr. gives his "I Have a Dream" speech.

EPILOGUE

*C*ome years later, we saw more terrible wars; we saw leaders like Dr. King, Malcolm Shabazz, and Bobby Kennedy shot and killed by people who, as Dr. King put it, "cannot disagree without being disagreeable." We watched cities burn, a man walk on the moon, presidents impeached, the Berlin Wall come down, millions more Americans march on Washington; we followed controversial elections and watched broken levees drown most of a city. There'd be plenty of trouble in the world, but a lot of joy, too.

Black folks began to do things that only decades before we hadn't dreamed of. African American generals commanded great armies for the first time. Black mayors and governors were elected in large cities. There were black principals of integrated schools, managers and owners of major professional sports teams. African American writers, actors, and directors won Nobel Prizes and Academy Awards. And we saw the first black Supreme Court justices and astronauts. There were plenty of firsts, honey. But the best was saved for last.

Forty-five years after Dr. King spoke on the steps of the Lincoln Memorial, I marched my old legs to the polls along with millions of other Americans to vote in an historic election. It was the first time that an African American—Barack Obama—had won the Democratic nomination and appeared on the national ballot for president of the United States. As I cast my vote, I thought about my grandfather Pap, who didn't live to see this moment, and my three children and two brothers, who did; I thought about my mother and father, and my aunts and uncles; I thought about Abe Lincoln, Frederick Douglass, and Harriet Tubman; I thought about presidents Kennedy and Johnson, Dr. King, Thurgood Marshall, the Freedom Riders, the marchers, and all of the people who lived and died so that I might walk into this booth and cast my vote. I thought about them all and smiled; and as I walked away, I closed my eyes and said, "Thank you."

Our centuries-long struggle for freedom and equal rights had helped make the American promise of life, liberty, and the pursuit of happiness a reality for all Americans. We have come a mighty long way, honey, and we still have a good ways to go, but that promise and the right to fight for it is worth every ounce of its weight in gold. It is our nation's heart and soul.

Voting poll, Chicago, 2008

AUTHOR'S NOTE

It's ironic. History was not at all my favorite subject in school, and yet as a full-time artist and author, for almost a decade I've found myself primarily writing about and illustrating historical subjects. I've loved painting subjects like slavery, the Underground Railroad, and the civil rights movement, but never had I pieced them together in a single volume. The idea of doing this was exciting because it gave me an opportunity to delve deeper into the story of America, learn its history from the ground up, and see it through the eyes of the people who lived it. As I read, wrote, sketched, and painted during the creation of *Heart and Soul*, the American story came alive to me.

Painting historical American subjects pushes me to learn more about who I am, where I come from, and the role my ancestors played in helping form our country. Before working on *Heart and Soul*, I had known that African Americans had a deep connection to America, but it wasn't until I became engrossed in my research that I could fully appreciate how. I learned that whether willingly or unwillingly, African Americans and Europeans forged a new country together. And their interdependent relationship is what would sustain the new country and allow it to thrive. Although our beginnings were not free of blemish, the work of navigating through the marvelous words of the Declaration of Independence and the contradictory inhumane and discriminatory practices of the new country would help define the nation's character over the span of hundreds of years. It is a story of the country's continuing challenges of coming-of-age.

I knew I could not convey the *whole* story in a hundred pages, so I felt the most natural and concise way to tell the tale would be through the recollections of a narrator whose family history was very closely tied to the American story. I first thought of my own family and began interviewing some of the eldest members who had lived through key moments in our history. I heard stories about the last slaves in my family and my great-great-grandmother who was a member of the Seminole Nation. I learned of those in my family who had come from the Deep South and made the trip northward to escape Jim Crow or find work in northern cities during and after the great wars. I found worn photos of great-aunts and great-uncles who proudly posed for the camera as they stood in front of a cornfield or in their military uniforms. I listened to aunts and uncles describe what it was like during a college sit-in or when they heard Dr. Martin Luther King Jr. speak in their hometown. Through the memories of my elders, the American story unfolded right before my eyes. I wanted to share these stories in the way that I heard and saw them, through the words and family photos of an elder African American, a grandmother-like figure who would allow me to focus on major historical milestones that affected both her family and the rest of the country. So when the narrator describes her family's journey from Virginia to Chicago and their celebration when they crossed the Mason-Dixon Line, we understand the importance of this moment as a personal achievement for her family, but at the same time we also learn about the Great Migration and how it literally changed the face of America.

Heart and Soul is not only the story of my family, but an intimate introduction to American history that I hope will remind readers of our extraordinary story and inspire them to learn more about America as I have done—by exploring their unique family stories and their connection to the American story.

TIME LINE

1565—African Americans first arrive in North America as slaves of Spanish colonists.

1619—The first English colony in North America, Virginia, begins importing Africans as slaves.

December 16, 1773—American colonists protest British authority and dump over three hundred chests of tea into Boston Harbor in an act more commonly known as the Boston Tea Party.

1775—The American Revolutionary War begins.

July 4, 1776—The Declaration of Independence is signed, proclaiming the thirteen American colonies as independent states, free from the rule of the British Empire.

September 3, 1783—Britain signs the Treaty of Paris, signifying the formal end of the American Revolutionary War.

June 21, 1788—The Constitution of the United States of America is ratified.

April 30, 1789—General George Washington is inaugurated as the first president of the United States of America.

1793—Construction of the Capitol, Washington, DC, begins.

March 1807—Reacting to British pressure, the United States outlaws the African slave trade; however, slavery is not abolished internally nor is the domestic slave trade halted.

1817–1842—The United States engages in the First and Second Seminole Wars in Florida, with many Seminoles forced to relocate west of the Mississippi.

February 1818—Frederick Douglass is born into slavery.

Circa 1820—Harriet Tubman is born into slavery.

September 3, 1838—On his third attempt, Frederick Douglass escapes from the plantation and flees to New York.

1845—Frederick Douglass publishes his best-known work, *Narrative of the Life of Frederick Douglass, an American Slave.*

September 17, 1849—Harriet Tubman and her brother escape from slavery.

September 18, 1850—Congress passes the Fugitive Slave Act of 1850, declaring that any runaway slave, if captured, should be returned to his or her owner.

Circa 1859—Slaves begin singing and passing along the song "Follow the Drinking Gourd," a song whose lyrics contained a road map for the Underground Railroad.

1850–1860s—The Underground Railroad, established earlier in the nineteenth century, is at its peak.

1854—Congress passes the Kansas-Nebraska Act, allowing settlers of new territories to decide whether or not to allow slavery.

March 6, 1857—The Dred Scott decision is announced, and the Supreme Court rules that people of African descent imported into the United States and held as slaves and their descendants are not protected by the Constitution and cannot be naturalized U.S. citizens.

December 20, 1860–February 1, 1861—South Carolina, Mississippi, Florida, Alabama, Georgia, Louisiana, and Texas secede from the Union. The Confederate States are formed in February 1861.

March 4, 1861—Abraham Lincoln is inaugurated the sixteenth president of the United States.

April 12, 1861—Fort Sumter, South Carolina, is attacked by Confederate troops; the Civil War begins.

April 17, 1861–May 20, 1861—Virginia, Arkansas, Tennessee, and North Carolina secede from the Union and join the Confederate States.

1862—African Americans are allowed to officially join the Union army.

January 1, 1863—President Lincoln issues the Emancipation Proclamation, formally freeing slaves from states that do not rejoin the Union.

April 9, 1865—Confederate General Robert E. Lee surrenders to the Union; the Civil War ends.

April 15, 1865—Abraham Lincoln is assassinated by John Wilkes Booth. Andrew Johnson assumes the presidency.

December 6, 1865—The Thirteenth Amendment to the United States Constitution is adopted, officially abolishing slavery and involuntary servitude.

1865—The Ku Klux Klan forms.

March 2, 1867–March 11, 1868—Congress passes four statutes, known as the Reconstruction Acts.

March 2, 1867—Howard University, the first historically black university, is chartered.

February 3, 1870—The Fifteenth Amendment to the United States Constitution is adopted, granting black men the right to vote. This amendment was part of the Reconstruction Acts.

February 23, 1870—The first black U.S.

congressman, Hiram Rhodes Revels, is elected to the United States Senate.

July 12, 1872—Elijah McCoy invents and patents a lubricating cup that oils the gears of train engines. The product is so superb that engineers only want "the real McCoy."

1876—Congress begins enacting Jim Crow laws, which mandate that everything be divided by race, including public education, transportation, restrooms, restaurants, and drinking fountains. The Jim Crow laws are based on the notion of "separate but equal."

July 4, 1881—Booker T. Washington spearheads the founding of the Tuskegee Institute, which opens its doors on this day.

1883—Jan Ernst Matzeliger invents and patents a machine that makes the production of shoes more cost-effective and efficient.

October 16, 1901—President Theodore Roosevelt hosts Booker T. Washington for dinner at the White House.

1910–1930—Blacks begin the "Great Migration," moving from the South to northern cities like New York, Chicago, Philadelphia, and Detroit in hopes of obtaining factory work.

June 28, 1914—Archduke Franz Ferdinand, next in line to the throne of the Austro-Hungarian empire, is assassinated. World War I begins.

1917—The United States enters World War I.

1918—World War I ends.

August 19, 1920—The Nineteenth Amendment to the United States Constitution is ratified, granting voting rights to women.

January 15, 1929—Martin Luther King Jr. is born.

October 29, 1929—The U.S. stock market crashes. The Great Depression begins.

June 19, 1936—American boxer Joe Louis fights German boxer Max Schmeling for the first time. Louis is knocked out in the twelfth round.

June 22, 1938—Boxer Joe Louis wins a rematch bout against Max Schmeling. Louis knocks out Schmeling in the first round.

1939—George Washington Carver receives the Roosevelt Medal for Outstanding Contribution to Southern Agriculture.

1939—Adolf Hitler invades Poland. World War II begins.

1941—United States naval base at Pearl Harbor is bombed by the Japanese. President Franklin Delano Roosevelt declares war on Japan, and the United States officially enters World War II.

1944—The Tuskegee Airmen (the 332nd) and the 761st Tank Battalion are put into combat action.

September 2, 1945—World War II officially ends.

April 15, 1947—Jackie Robinson becomes the first black man to play in Major League Baseball since the 1880s.

May 17, 1954—In the Brown v. Board of Education of Topeka decision, the Supreme Court rules that the segregation of education is unconstitutional, granting the right for black children to attend school with white children. Integration begins.

December 1, 1955—Rosa Parks refuses to move from her bus seat on a segregated bus. She is arrested. Led by Dr. Martin Luther King Jr., the black community of Montgomery, Alabama, boycotts the buses for a total of three hundred eighty-one days.

September 4, 1957—In Little Rock, Arkansas, nine black children are blocked by the Arkansas National Guard from entering their school, Central High School. On September 24, President Dwight D. Eisenhower orders the army to escort them into the building.

February 1, 1960—Four black students protest Jim Crow laws by sitting at the whites only counter at the Greensboro, North Carolina, Woolworth's. They are arrested.

May 1963—Six hundred students protesting Jim Crow laws in Birmingham, Alabama, led by Martin Luther King Jr., are attacked by police dogs and sprayed with fire hoses in Kelly Ingram Park.

August 28, 1963—Dr. Martin Luther King Jr. delivers his famous "I Have a Dream" speech on the Washington Mall.

July 2, 1964—President Lyndon Johnson signs the Civil Rights Act into law, prohibiting discrimination based on race, color, religion, sex, and national origin.

April 4, 1968—Martin Luther King Jr. is assassinated. James Earl Ray confesses to the murder two months later.

January 20, 2009—Barack Hussein Obama, the forty-fourth president of the United States, is sworn into office. He is the country's first black president.

BIBLIOGRAPHY

Africans in America: America's Journey Through Slavery. DVD. WGBH Boston, 1998.

American Experience: Citizen King. DVD. PBS, 2004.

American Experience: TR: The Story of Theodore Roosevelt. DVD. PBS, 2006.

Baker, John F., Jr. *The Washingtons of Wessyngton Plantation: Stories of My Family's Journey to Freedom*. New York: Atria, 2009.

Berlin, Ira, Marc Favreau, and Steven F. Miller, eds. *Remembering Slavery: African Americans Talk About Their Personal Experiences of Slavery and Emancipation*. New York: The New Press, 1998.

Black Sorority Project: The Exodus. DVD. Derek & Jamar Productions, 2006.

Burns, Ken. *The War*. DVD. PBS, 2007.

Chafe, William H., Raymond Gavins, and Robert Korstad, eds. *Remembering Jim Crow: African Americans Tell About Life in the Segregated South*. New York: The New Press, 2008.

Davis, Kenneth C. *America's Hidden History: Untold Tales of the First Pilgrims, Fighting Women, and Forgotten Founders Who Shaped a Nation*. New York: Harper Collins, 2008.

———. *Don't Know Much About History: Everything You Need to Know About American History but Never Learned*. New York: Avon Books, 2004.

Editors of TIME Magazine. *TIME America: An Illustrated History*. New York: Time, 2007.

Ellis, Joseph J. *American Creation: Triumphs and Tragedies in the Founding of the Republic*. New York: Knopf, 2007.

Equiano, Olaudah. *The Interesting Narrative and Other Writings*. Rev. ed. New York: Penguin Classics, 2003.

Franklin, John Hope, and Evelyn Brooks Higginbottom. *From Slavery to Freedom: A History of African Americans*. New York: Alfred A. Knopf, 2000.

Freedman, Russell. *Who Was First?: Discovering the Americas*. New York: Clarion Books, 2007.

Goodwin, Doris Kearns. *Team of Rivals: The Political Genius of Abraham Lincoln*. New York: Simon & Schuster, 2006.

The History Channel Presents: Voices of the Civil Rights Movement. DVD. New Video Group, Inc., New York, 2006.

Huggins, Nathan Irvin. *Black Odyssey: The African-American Ordeal in Slavery*. New York: Vintage Books, 1990.

Kagan, Neil, and Stephen G. Hyslop. *Eyewitness to the Civil War: The Complete History from Secession to Reconstruction*. Washington, DC: National Geographic Books, 2006.

Katz, William Loren. *The Black West: A Documentary and Pictorial History of the African American Role in the Westward Expansion of the United States*. New York: Harlem Moon/Broadway Books, 2005.

Lardas, Mark. *African American Soldier in the American Civil War: USCT 1862-66*. New York: Osprey Publishing, 2006.

Levine, Ellen. *Freedom's Children: Young Civil Rights Activists Tell Their Own Stories*. New York: Puffin Books, 2000.

Morrow, Willie L. *400 Years Without a Comb: The Untold Story*. San Diego: Morrow's Unlimited Inc., 1973.

Philbrick, Nathaniel. *Mayflower: A Story of Courage, Community, and War*. New York: Penguin (Non-Classics), 2007.

The Real George Washington. DVD. National Geographic, 2009.

Stewart, Julia. *African Proverbs and Wisdom: A Collection for Every Day of the Year, From More Than Forty African Nations*. New York: Kensington, 2002.

Still, William. *The Underground Railroad: Authentic Narratives and First-Hand Accounts*. Mineola, NY: Dover Publications, 2007.

Zinn, Howard. *A People's History of the United States: 1492 to Present*. New York: Harper Perennial Modern Classics, 1995.

INDEX

DISCUSSION QUESTIONS

1. Who is speaking in the prologue, and who is the "honey" whom she is addressing? Why did the author choose to tell this history through the voice of a narrator addressing someone she cares about? CCSS.RL.4-8.5

2. Why is Chapter 1 titled "Declarations of Independence" in the plural? How did most African Americans come to this country, and why were they not encouraged in the beginning of the Revolution to fight in the Continental Army? CCSS.RI.4-8.1

3. Discuss the statement "It would be a long while before we figured out that we could not win our freedom with our fists or guns. We would have to find another way." [p. 21] How did the institution of slavery force the people into submission? CCSS.RI.4-8.3

4. Why didn't the writers of the U.S. Constitution stop slavery after founding this country? What points might have come up in a debate among the delegates to the Constitutional Convention? Discuss William Lloyd Garrison's quote: "That which is not just is not law." [p. 23] CCSS.RI.4-8.1, 3

5. Discuss the events leading up to the Civil War. Why did slavery end in the North but continue in the South? Why did it take so long for black soldiers to be allowed to fight in the Union Army? Why do you think "Pap" returned to his old plantation after the war? CCSS.RI.4-8.1, 3

6. Discuss the Reconstruction Era after the Civil War and why it represented a virtual return to slavery conditions for most African Americans. What were the causes of the failure of Reconstruction? What were Jim Crow laws, and how did they affect the social life of a community? CCSS.RI.4-8.3, 4

7. Discuss the connection between African Americans and Native Americans. What aspects of their lives did they have in common? What were the differences in their experiences with European settlers on this continent? CCSS.RI.4-8.3

8. What effect did the Great Migration have on the lives of African Americans? Why did so many leave their homes? What were the challenges they faced in their new communities? CCSS.RI.4-8.1, 2

9. Discuss the importance of the arts to African Americans in the early twentieth century. Why is this period different from the one before? In what ways did the African American experience begin to influence the arts in America? CCSS.RI.4-8.8

10. Why was the boxing match between Joe Louis and Max Schmeling so important to people around the world? Discuss the quote from Jackie Robinson: "I learned that I was in two wars, one against the foreign enemy, the other against prejudice at home." [p. 71] How did the experience of fighting in World War II change the people who returned from it? How did it change the country? What does the narrator mean when she says, "Jim Crow's days were numbered"? [p. 77] CCSS.RI.4-8.3

11. What does the narrator call "the most important idea ever introduced to America by an African American"? [p. 80] Why is this idea more important than scientific discoveries? Discuss the impact of Dr. Martin Luther King, Jr.'s ideas on African Americans and on the history of his time. Why was he unique? CCSS.RI.4-8.2, 3

12. Why is the last chapter titled "Revolution"? Compare the Civil Rights Movement in the 1950s and 1960s to the American Revolution in 1776. How are these social upheavals similar? Why did it take nearly two hundred years for the rights of African Americans to catch up to white Americans? Is the revolution over? Why does the narrator say that the Civil Rights Bill of 1964 was the "beginning of a new struggle for every American"? [p. 95] CCSS.RI.4-8.2, 3, 4

CLASSROOM ACTIVITIES

1. **The Voyage Was Rough.** Draw a map of the routes that were taken by slave ships from Africa to the Americas. Indicate on your map the different countries in Africa from which people were kidnapped and sold as slaves. Show on your map what was known as "triangle trade" and how it worked during the days of transatlantic slave trade in the eighteenth and early nineteenth centuries. CCSS.RI.4-8.7

2. **Let Freedom Ring.** Read more about one of the key figures in the fight to free the slaves—Lincoln, Douglass, Tubman, etc. Write a character sketch of that person and include their childhood experiences, as well as their adult life. What did you learn about this person that gave him or her the courage to fight for freedom? CCSS.RI.4-8.3, 6

3. **Forty Acres and a Mule.** List the causes of the failure of Reconstruction after the Civil War. Describe the practice of "sharecropping" and how it worked. List the reasons why it was so difficult for African Americans to become fully independent under this kind of work. CCSS.RI.4-8.1

4. **A New Kind of Life.** Write a letter from an African American boy or girl who took part in the Great Migration to a friend or relative who stayed behind in the South. What changes would that child notice—the sights, the community, the way of life, the effect on the family? Include the experience of the journey and how it felt after the family was settled. Write a return letter from the friend or family member in the South describing their life and experiences there. CCSS.W.4-8.3

5. **A Renaissance of the Arts.** Read a story or a collection of poems by one of the writers of the Harlem Renaissance—Langston Hughes, Zora Neale Hurston, James Weldon Johnson, or another. Write about the emotions

expressed in this piece and how it makes you feel as you read it today. What can you learn about the writer's life experience that was expressed in his or her work? CCSS. RL.4-8.5 and CCSS.W.4-8.9

6. **The Sporting Life.** Research the life story of an historic African American sports star of the early twentieth century—Jesse Owens, Joe Louis, Jackie Robinson, Wilma Rudolph, or another. Write a short biography about the athlete's life experiences, the prejudice he or she faced, and the way he or she overcame obstacles in a quest for excellence. Present your subject to the class by telling his or her story in your own words. CCSS.W.4-8.7 and CCSS.SL.4-8.4

7. **Necessity is the Mother of Invention.** Make a chart of the inventions and discoveries made by African Americans. Many of them are listed on pages 79 and 80, but you can find others by researching. Choose one of these inventions or discoveries and learn more about the inventor and the process he or she followed. What was the impact of this invention on other people? Why is it important to know about these inventors? CCSS.RI.4-8.7

AN INTERVIEW WITH KADIR NELSON

1. *How did you decide on the voice for the narrator?*

When conceiving the voice of the narrator, I thought of many of the people in my life whose soothing voices and wonderful stories I loved to hear again and again. People like my grandmother, my mother, my aunts and uncles, and friends like Walt McCoy, Debbie Allen, and Jerdine Nolen. I interviewed them and then rolled all their voices into one, that of an elder, a one-hundred-year-old African American woman whose family history would be closely tied to the history of America.

I wanted to hear the story of America as if it were just that, a story, so the narrator speaks to readers as if she were their grandmother. It makes this incredibly expansive history very intimate.

2. *What part of the history did you find most difficult to write about and illustrate?*

I found World War I to be a bit tricky to write about because it was a very highly politicized and convoluted affair that most people really didn't and still don't understand. Writing about it in a way that was honest and true to the character telling the story and also engaging to young readers was no simple task. It's almost like trying to explain America's role in Vietnam or Iraq in a simple way. There are a lot of moving parts.

The biggest challenge I faced when creating the art was the sheer number of paintings I had to create to tell the story—almost fifty paintings! I still marvel at that number.

3. *What part of the history did you most enjoy writing about and illustrating?*

I enjoyed writing about Pap and his journey most of all. His life was probably the most varied and transformative of all in the narrator's family. He was born in Africa and captured at a very young age, and then brought to America and made a slave. He escaped as a young man and then fought with the Union in the Civil War. After the war, Pap became a Buffalo Soldier out west where he met his wife, Sarah, a member of the Seminole nation. He returned to the South and became a sharecropper and then moved north with his family during what would later be called the Great Migration, working alongside the masses of African Americans who contributed to the war effort. Pap's journey truly is the story of early African Americans in the United States.

Out of all the paintings in the book, I most enjoyed painting Pap's portrait as a young child.

4. *How did you choose specific incidents to write about and illustrate? How much did you rely on family stories and how much on research to depict different eras?*

When composing this story, I knew I had to write about major milestones in the American story: the American Revolution, slavery, the Civil War, Reconstruction, etc., as well as intimate family stories from the narrator's family history. I would address how these incidences, large and small, affected the narrator's family and the rest of the country.

Many of the narrator's family stories came from my interviewing elder family members on both sides of my family and historical interviews conducted by others. Pap's name came from my aunt's aunt, Gaynell Taylor.

The story about black-eyed peas comes from my great-great-grandfather who forbade his descendants from eating them on New Year's Day. Or former slaves' eye-witness accounts of Civil War battles—stories like these made this history much more real to me.

5. *What changes do you think need to occur in America in the next one hundred years? What new chapters would you want a future historian to be able to add to this story?*

If I had any say about how things should go, I'd hope that racism, nationalism, and classism were things of the past. It's a tall order, but it's not impossible. With each new generation, racism loses its footing, and as the world grows smaller with the World Wide Web and easier travel, other barriers may fall.

Discussion guide created by Connie Rockman,
Youth Literature Consultant and adjunct professor
of children's and young adult literature.